RUGBY

Facts, Figures & Fun

*"Any book without a mistake in it has had
too much money spent on it"*
Sir William Collins, publisher

RUGBY

Facts, Figures & Fun

Liam McCann

ff&f

Rugby
Facts, Figures & Fun

Published by
Facts, Figures & Fun, an imprint of
AAPPL Artists' and Photographers' Press Ltd.
Church Farm House, Wisley, Surrey GU23 6QL
info@ffnf.co.uk www.ffnf.co.uk
info@aappl.com www.aappl.com

Sales and Distribution
UK and export: Turnaround Publisher Services Ltd.
orders@turnaround-uk.com
USA and Canada: Sterling Publishing Inc.
sales@sterlingpub.com
Australia & New Zealand: Peribo Pty.
peribomec@bigpond.com
South Africa: Trinity Books. trinity@iafrica.com

A catalogue record for this book is available
from the British Library.

ISBN 13: 9781904332541
ISBN 10: 1904332544

Design (contents and cover): Malcolm Couch
mal.couch@blueyonder.co.uk

Printed in China by Imago Publishing
info@imago.co.uk

CONTENTS

RUGBY

THE NAME

The sport of rugby derives its name from the town and school in Warwickshire where William Webb Ellis was a pupil. It is believed that in 1823 he picked up a football and "with fine disregard for the rules of the sport, took the ball in his arms and ran with it", thus originating the game's distinctive handling feature. However, there seems to be little factual evidence to support this story. Indeed it is based on an account sent to the school magazine in 1876 by Matthew Bloxham, a student at Rugby with Webb Ellis, who told of an event his brother had witnessed.

THE GAME

Primitive forms of the game had been played for hundreds of years (notably in Ireland where the 1527 Statute of Galway allowed football but banned an early form of hurling called hokie), though the innovation of being allowed to run with the ball was certainly a turning point. In fact Webb Ellis's father, stationed in Ireland with the Dragoons, would have noticed locals playing the game of *Caid* (meaning scrotum of the bull) in either its field (the ball must pass between two marked trees) or cross-country (the ball must cross a parish boundary) forms. The Welsh believe field *Caid* derived from their *Criapan*, which the Cornish called Hurling to Goales, and dated back to the bronze age.

It wasn't just in Britain that this game of throwing a ball to gain territory was evolving. The French called their pastime *La Soule* (a pig or cow's bladder filled with oil and covered in leather) and the Vikings *Knappan*, while similar games existed throughout the Pacific islands, Polynesia and even amongst the Eskimos. By the sixth century the Romans had developed a sport called *Harpastum* meaning 'the small ball game', but this probably derived independently from games passed across Asia.

William Fitzstephen, a monk, noted in his history of London a game of ball being played in 1175, with the city's youth turning out on Shrove Tuesday. Edward II passed a law in 1314 forbidding Londoners from participating in the somewhat dangerous derivative, the sport of football, in which opponents used a variety of tactics (stamping, hacking) to kick or carry a ball past one another. Later kings continued to suppress the sport as it prevented people from practicing archery, a far more valuable skill. Then, in 1424, James I of Scotland decreed "that na man play at the fute bali." Indeed this sentiment was echoed by nine monarchs across Europe with anyone caught playing facing fines or imprisonment. The game was outlawed again by a number of kings and queens before being formally introduced to schools in the middle of the 18th Century.

The game of football that developed under its own Rugby rules was played at the school between 1750 and 1823. Although handling the ball was permitted, players were not allowed to run with it. Sometimes as many as a hundred players took to the field for each side!

If Webb Ellis picked up the ball and ran, he would have done so at considerable personal risk as the game was quite violent, and the practice was not widely acceptable until officially legalised in the laws of the game in 1845. However, some school reports mention Jem Mackie running powerfully with the ball in hand in 1838, and Bigside Levee (a collection of sixth formers) writing a list of rules permitting the practice.

While both the kicking and running forms of this ball game were being outlawed by the Highways Act of 1835, which forbade their playing on public land by the common man, they found refuge in schools, and different laws sprung up according to where you played. Why the rules laid down at Rugby School have survived while those from Cheltenham, Shrewsbury and Marlborough did not is unclear, but it seems likely that Rugby's influential headmaster Dr Thomas Arnold lobbied for their laws to be universally applied. By the mid 1860s many schools abided by the Rugby rules.

As pupils left school and went to university they took the game with them. Old Rugbeians challenged Old Etonians to a game of football at Cambridge university in 1839, with the Rugbeians using their hands to secure victory. As a result, representatives from the major public schools at Cambridge met to draw up the Cambridge rules of 1848. In 1863 another meeting outlawed hacking and tripping. Then, in 1871, three Old Rugbeians and Edwin Ash of Richmond called a meeting of 21 clubs – to be chaired by Richmond captain E.C.Holmes – at the Pall Mall restaurant in Regent Street, and together they formed the Rugby Football Union.

FOUNDER MEMBERS OF THE RFU

Harlequins, Blackheath, Guy's Hospital,
Civil Service, Wellington College, King's College,
St Paul's, Gipsies, Flamingos, Mohicans,
Wimbledon Hornets, Marlborough Nomads,
West Kent, Law, Lausanne,
Addison, Belsize Park, Ravenscourt Park,
Chapham Rovers, Queen's House

The 1870s saw the game spread around the world, first to
Australia and New Zealand and then to Canada and the
United States. In 1875, British troops stationed in Cape
Town introduced the game to South Africa. It was during
this period that the formations changed markedly.
Numbers were reduced to 15-a-side, usually ten forwards
and five backs. As the game changed in England, it also
spawned variants abroad. In the USA the scrum was
replaced with the line of scrimmage and forward passes
were allowed, while in Ireland football and rugby merged
to form Gaelic football, a fifteen man game involving
kicking and running with the ball in hand. Played
predominantly in Melbourne, rugby also evolved to
produce the popular Australian Rules variant.

——— AMERICAN FOOTBALL ———

The National Collegiate Athletic Association (NCAA)
drew up a set of 61 rules for the game in 1876, and
though they remain largely unchanged today, some minor
differences can be found between college football, professional football and other variants, such as Canadian
Football. Play is usually stop-start with the ball going
dead for extended periods in the professional game
(which can last for up to four hours). Each team must

attempt to move the ball ten or more yards up-field using a succession of four 'downs'. If successful, they gain another set of four, otherwise the ball is handed to the opposition. A team must carry the ball into their opponent's end zone to score a touchdown.

Main differences

	Rugby	American Football
Pitch size	Max 144 x 69 metres	120 x 53 1/3 yards
Match length	2 x 40 minute halves	4 x 15 minute quarters
Half time	10 minutes	15 minutes
Number of players on the pitch	15 (Union), 13 (League)	11
Substitutes	5 from 7 (Union), 4 interchange (League)	Up to 33
Direction of passes	Lateral or backwards	Any, behind first down line. Lateral or backwards thereafter
Scoring system	See tables	Touchdown: 6 points, conversion: 1, field goal: 3, safety: 2
Protective clothing allowed	Shoulder pads plus joint strapping and head guards	Helmet, shoulder pads, chest protectors, thigh pads
Set plays	Scrum, lineout (Union), Scrum, play-the-ball (League)	Line of scrimmage, blitz defence
Ball shape	Oval	Oval
Officials	1 referee, 2 linesmen, 1 video replay official	1 referee plus 6 on field assistants and video replay officials

——— GAELIC FOOTBALL ———

The field game predates rugby by some time but it wasn't until 1884 that the Gaelic Athletic Association (GAA) was formed, and not until 1887 that the game was codified. There are now some 2500 clubs in Ireland, the best 32 of which annually contest the Sam Maguire trophy for the right to be called All-Ireland champions. The ball must be hit by hand or fist (not thrown) in the Gaelic and Australian variants, and in the Gaelic it may be passed in any direction in order to score a goal in a net under the rugby-style H posts, or a point if it crosses above the bar.

——— AUSTRALIAN RULES ———

A letter by Tom Wills in *Bell's Life in Victoria and Sporting Chronicle* in July 1858 called for a football match—and a code of laws to govern it—to ensure that their cricketers kept fit during the winter. The first match was played at the end of the month at Yarra Park next to the Melbourne Cricket Ground (MCG). Wills then drew up a set of laws based on some elements evident from the first few games and others drawn from the Aboriginal game of *Marn Grook*, which included the spectacular high mark, or speccie. There is no offside rule in Australian Football, and no limitation on ball or player movement, but the need to bounce the ball every 15 metres probably derives from the Gaelic law whereby a player must bounce every four steps to retain possession. Once within range of the four scoring posts (each 6.4 metres apart) any player may kick the ball between the taller centre posts for a goal, or between the centre and shorter outer posts for a behind.

Main differences

	Gaelic Football	Aussie Rules
Pitch size:	130-145 x 80-90 metres	Oval. 135-185 x 110-155 metres
Match length:	2 x 30 or 2 x 35 minutes	4 x 20 minute quarters
Half time:	10 minutes	20 minutes max
Number of players on the pitch:	15	18
Substitutes:	6 from 15	4
Direction of passes:	Any, by hand/fist or foot	Any, by hand/fist or foot
Scoring system:	Goal: 3 points, point: 1	Goal: 6 points, behind: 1 point
Protective clothing allowed:	Usually none	For medical purposes only
Set plays:	Sidelines, kickouts	Ball-up, free kick
Ball shape:	Round: 68-70 cm	Oval
Officials:	Referee, 2 linesmen, 4 umpires	3 field umpires, 2 boundary umpires, 2 goal umpires, 2 timekeepers

The Great Schism

With the game of rugby growing rapidly, the need to pay players who missed work on Saturdays became an issue. Players in Lancashire argued that as cricketers and footballers were offered so-called 'broken time' payments as compensation, so should they. By 1893 clubs in Yorkshire were openly paying players and were charged with professionalism. This led, somewhat inevitably, to a battle between the two sides, those who wished to remain strictly amateur, and those who did not.

Rugby Timeline

Bronze Age-1175 AD: Various games are played around the world whereby one team must carry a leather sack across a goal line. The most common appears to be the Celtic game of *Caid*.

1175: Monks document the first game of ball in London.

1314: Edward II passes a statute forbidding Londoners to play ball.

1365: Edward III orders his sheriffs to suppress the game in favour of archery.

1388: Richard II again forbids playing ball.

1424: James I of Scotland debars the 'fute bali'.

1457: James II introduces an Act of Parliament disallowing the sport.

1545-1660: Henry VIII, Elizabeth I and Charles II enact laws banning the game.

1750: Football introduced to Rugby School. Players may handle, but must not run with, the ball.

1807: William Webb Ellis born in Salford, Manchester.

1810: Kiwi Chief Te Rauparaha performs the first 'haka' to avoid being killed by his enemy.

1816: Webb Ellis enrols at Rugby school.

1820-23: At some point the game changes, with the ball being carried in the hands.

1835: Highways Act forbids the game being played outside schools.

1839: Old Rugbeians and Old Etonians clash at Cambridge University.

1841: Rugby rules officially allow running with the ball provided a) the ball was caught cleanly, b) the catcher was not offside and c) the catcher did not immediately pass.

1843: First rugby club formed by Guy's Hospital.

1845: W.D. Arnold, W.W. Shirley and F. Hutchins submit 37 rules of the game to the Sixth Levee. Length of game, fair catches, knock-ons, offsides and drop outs defined.

1848: Rugby, Eton, Harrow, Marlborough, Westminster and Shrewsbury meet to draw up the Cambridge Rules.

1851: William Gilbert makes the first Rugby School Football, an oval ball inflated by a pig's bladder.

1853: 25 yard line established.

1854: Students at Trinity College, Dublin, claim their club is the world's first.

1857: Though the final score is not recorded, five goals occur in a match between Rugby and the rest of the world at Liverpool RFU. Richard Sykes, captain of football at Rugby, provides the ball. He later forms the town of Sykeston, North Dakota, and is credited with exporting the game to America.

1858: Edinburgh Academicals FC become the first Scottish club side. Ned Haig, who later invents rugby sevens, is born.

1863: First recorded club game between Richmond and Blackheath becomes the oldest regular fixture. 11 clubs meet as the football association (FA) in London. It is planned to merge rugby and football rules to bring about a common game. Blackheath withdraw in protest at the outlawing of running with the ball and hacking. Many other clubs follow their lead, and the new laws define the game of soccer, a predominantly dribbling sport. On December 19 Barnes FC play Richmond in the first game under FA rules. Richmond then withdraw from the FA.

1864: Sydney University become the first Australian club.

1868: Montreal becomes first Canadian club. Richmond calls for a ban on hacking.

1870: Lancashire defeat Yorkshire in first county match. Charles Monro brings the game to New Zealand. Nelson College take on Nelson FC in the first match. Richard Lindon invents the inflatable rubber bladder which replaces the traditional pig's bladder inside the ball.

1871: The RFU forms in the Pall Mall restaurant, with Algernon Rutter elected as its first president. Rutter, along with E.C. Holmes and L.J. Maton (all lawyers), formulate the first set of rules (laws), which are approved in June. West of Scotland FC promote the first international (Scotland versus England) at Raeburn Place in Edinburgh in front of 4000 fans. Scotland win the 20-a-side 100 minute match by a goal and a try to a single goal. England gain revenge the following year at the Oval.

1872: William Webb Ellis dies in Menton, France. The first Oxford-Cambridge 'Varsity' match is played. Oxford win by a goal to nil.

1874: Harvard play Montreal's McGill University in the first American match. Rugby is played in Cape Town for the first time. A referee is appointed to control the match while the two umpires patrol the sidelines.

1875: First England-Ireland match. Shortly afterwards the number of players is reduced to 15. There are usually ten forwards, two attacking half-backs and three defensive backs. Some teams swap a defensive back for an attacking half-back, and he becomes the first three-quarter. Cardiff develop a short passing move to the flying half-back. This is later shortened to fly-half.

1877: England beat Ireland by two goals and two tries to nil in the first 15-a-side international.

1878: Broughton play Swinton under floodlights in Salford, Manchester.

1880: England beat Scotland by two goals and three tries to one goal to win the Calcutta Cup for the first time. In the USA the scrum is replaced by a loose line of forwards called the line of scrimmage. Scotland use three three-quarters against Ireland.

1881: Welsh Rugby Union founded by 11 clubs. England meet Wales for the first time and win 69-0 in modern scoring terms. Independent referees are used in internationals for the first time.

1882: Neutral referees introduced. Australian club New South Wales become the first team to tour when they take on New Zealand's provincial sides.

1883: The first sevens tournament held at Melrose Football Club in Scotland.

1884: European and Fijian soldiers bring the game to the smaller Pacific islands. In Scotland the Garryowen club is formed. It lends its name to the high kick, or up and under. Cardiff use four three-quarters.

1885: Referees are given whistles; umpires are given sticks, then flags.

1886: International Rugby Board founded by Ireland, Scotland and Wales.

1888: A British representative side tours Australia and New Zealand for the first time. Captain Bob Seddon is killed in a boating accident on the Hunter river. Kiwi captain Joe Warbrick later dies in a lava flow on Mount Tarawera.

1890: Despondent at the lack of rugby at the end of the season, W.P. Carpmael decides to assemble a side from the best players available—and the Barbarians are born. England becomes a member of the IRB.

1891: The British Isles win all 20 matches on their tour of South Africa.

1892: NZRFU formed.

1893: Poorer workers in the north of England are given 'broken time' payments to compensate their loss of earnings while playing rugby. At an emergency meeting at the Westminster Palace Hotel members from the county of Yorkshire propose paying players. G. Rowland Hill, secretary of the union, opposes the amendment. Referees are given sole responsibility of running the game. Wales win first Triple Crown by beating the other home unions.

1894: Try upgraded to three points, conversion dropped to two.

1895: 12 clubs resign from the Yorkshire Union to form a Northern Union. They wish to remain amateur but will accept 'broken time' payments. In all 22 clubs would join what became known as the Rugby League. The two sports then evolve separately, adopt new laws and become incompatible.

"If Englishmen call this playing, it would be impossible to say what they call fighting"
A Frenchman watching a game of football at
Derby in the 19th century

"He's missed three kicks so far, but by his own standards he'd have kicked every one"
Bill Beaumont

RUGBY UNION

Object of the Game

The aim of the game is to score more points than the opposition. Points are scored in a variety of ways.

The try: the ball must be touched down on or behind the opposition's goal-line using downward pressure from any part of the body between waist and neck, provided that the player controls the ball at the moment it is grounded.

The conversion: having scored a try the team may then attempt a kick at goal, provided the ball is placed on the field of play in line with where the try was scored. Points are awarded if it passes above the cross bar and between the posts.

The penalty: if a team contravenes a law to the point where the referee deems it to be foul play, he awards a penalty. If the posts are in range for the attacking team's kicker, they may try to kick a penalty goal.

The dropped goal: The ball is kicked from the hand in open play, provided that it bounces once before the player strikes it, and that it passes above the cross bar and between the posts.

CURRENT SCORING VALUES

YEAR	TRY	CONVERSION
Pre-1891	1	2
1891-1893	2	3
1893-1905	3	2
1905-1948	3	2
1948-1971	3	2
1971-1992	4	2
1992-	5	2

*A goal from mark allowed a defender a free kick at goal
from anywhere on the pitch provided he'd caught the ball

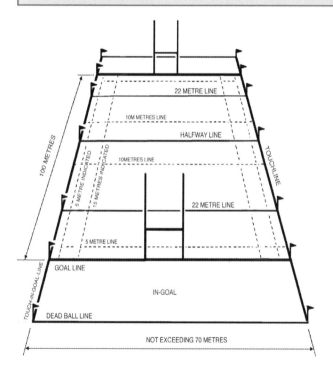

Penalty	Drop Goal	Goal from Mark*
2	3	3
3	4	4
3	4	4
3	4	3
3	3	3
3	3	Discontinued
3	3	

cleanly from the opposition's kick. It was dropped in 1971.

Until the game was codified the try was originally worth nothing, it merely allowed the attacking side a 'try' (kick) at the posts, which was worth points. (Some Rugby School old boys claim that when Webb Ellis picked up the ball and ran it over the line another player said, "That's not a goal, Ellis, but it was a nice try", though this story seems unlikely.)

—— Basic Laws of the Game ——

The game lasts for eighty minutes (two forty minute halves) plus any injury time, and is started after a toss of the coin with a drop kick from the halfway line. If the ball is caught cleanly by either side, the attacking team must move the ball forwards to score. This can be accomplished by running with the ball in hand, passing the ball laterally or backwards for another player to run with it, or kicking it from hand. Opposing players must attempt to halt the passage of the ball by tackling the player carrying it. A tackle will be deemed to be illegal if the defender does not use his arms, or grasps the ball carrier above the shoulders. If the attacker is tackled to ground, he or she must release the ball immediately and a 'ruck' forms. (The player doing the tackling must also roll away). If the player is stopped but remains standing, a 'maul' forms and the would-be tackler may lend his or her weight to that maul.

The Ruck

In open play the two teams must contest a grounded ball by driving over it to secure possession. Though the first person to arrive may attempt to collect the ball in hand, once there is more than one player from each side at the breakdown, they must bind together and use their feet to move the ball back towards their team—'rucking' the ball. Penalties are frequently awarded during this phase of play as it is common for players to try and slow the opposition's ball down illegally by using their hands or deliberately going to ground.

The Maul

In open play the teams contest a ball held in the hand by players on their feet. As with a ruck players must join the maul from their own side and attempt either to free the trapped ball or to move forwards by transferring it between players (a rolling maul) and varying the point of attack. The maul may move in any direction but if it stops the referee will award a scrum to the side initially defending (i.e. without the ball). The referee will also award a penalty against anyone trying to collapse the maul.

"Hey, Bill, there's a bird coming on with your bum on her chest"
England scrum-half Steve Smith lets captain Bill Beaumont know about Erica Roe's famous Twickenham streak

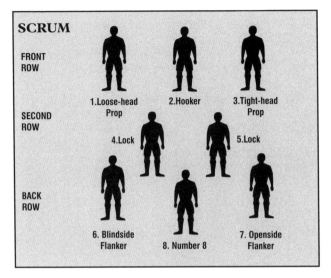

SCRUM

FRONT ROW

1.Loose-head Prop   2.Hooker   3.Tight-head Prop

SECOND ROW

4.Lock   5.Lock

BACK ROW

6. Blindside Flanker   8. Number 8   7. Openside Flanker

The Scrum

In open play if the ball is a) not caught cleanly and is knocked forwards at any time, or b) if an attacking player accidentally obstructs a defender, or c) if the ball does not carry ten metres from the kick off, the defending team are awarded a scrum. A scrum can also be awarded to the side going forward if the ball becomes lost in a ruck, or to the defensive side if it becomes static in a maul. A side awarded a penalty can also choose to tie up the opposition's forwards by opting to take a scrum instead. The team that is awarded the scrum usually retain the ball by virtue of the fact that a private signal can be given by the scrum-half or flanker as to when the ball is put in. The hookers must then strike for the ball and play it back to the number eight who may control it or release it to the scrum-half and the back-line. A scrum that is won by the defending side is said to have been taken 'against the head'.

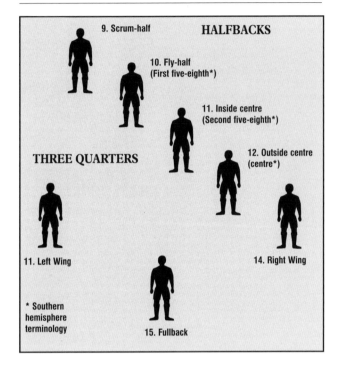

The scrum pits the eight forwards from each side in a set play. They pack down opposite one another in an effort to win the ball once it has been passed between them by the attacking scrum-half.

The main role of the forwards is to secure possession from either the set- or open plays and they are generally bigger and stronger – but slower as a consequence – than the backs. The main role of the back-line is to run with, and kick, the ball, and they are usually lighter, faster and more nimble, though less powerful. The backs (three-quarters) traditionally line up as shown above.

The Lineout

If the ball leaves the field on either side a lineout is called. The throw-in is awarded against the team that last touched the ball, unless the ball was kicked into touch following a penalty, in which case the team that kicked the ball retains the throw. The team throwing in may use any number of their forwards in the lineout, with the defending side being forced to match them. Both sets of forwards line up opposite the hooker who will throw the ball between the two packs. Players from both sides are lifted so that they might catch the ball and secure possession.

The Drop Out

This is similar to a restart kick but is taken from anywhere on or behind the defending 22-metre line. It usually occurs when an attacker kicks the ball into the defensive in-goal area and the ball is grounded by a defender. It can also occur if the attacking side kicks the ball dead and the defending side opt not to take a scrum from where the ball was kicked.

Offside

The offside rule is complex but there are a few key points. A player is deemed to be offside in open play if he or she participates in the game while standing in front of the player with the ball, or in front of a player who has kicked the ball. Players must retreat until they are onside (behind the ball player) before they may continue. If caught loitering, the referee will award a penalty. At set plays such as lineouts or scrums, an imaginary line across the pitch divides the two teams. Any player crossing this line, or any back approaching within ten metres of the lineout before the phase is complete, is also deemed to be offside.

Penalties

This is a punishment meted out by the referee for a deliberate infringement of the laws. If a player a) fails to release the ball after being tackled, b) enters a ruck or maul from the side, c) makes no effort to retreat to an onside position, d) tackles an opponent above the shoulders, or without the ball, e) obstructs a defender (crossing), f) fails to retreat ten metres or g) commits an act of serious foul play such as fighting, the referee will award a penalty. If the defending side complain to the referee, the official can move the penalty ten metres closer to their goal line.

The team awarded the penalty may a) kick at goal for three points, b) kick the ball into touch to receive the lineout throw, c) tap the ball for it to become live or d) take a scrum to tie up the opposition's forwards.

Free Kicks

The referee may award a free kick for a minor or non-deliberate offence such as time wasting or having an incorrect number of players at the lineout. The attacking side will usually decide to tap the ball to resume play or kick it into touch. No points can be scored and they will not be allowed the throw-in at the lineout.

"That's a better kick from Latham,
down towards the English halfway line"
Tim Horan

The Ball

The size and shape of the ball varied according to the dimensions of the pig's bladder that was used to make it. According to a reference in *Tom Brown's School Days* by Thomas Hughes, the ball had become oval by 1835. The bladder would have to be blown up through a clay pipe using lung power alone, an unpleasant task as it would still be in its green and smelly state. Thankfully, by 1870 rubber bladders were being supplied at a standard size, though the actual dimensions were not written into the laws until 1892. Over the next century there were minimal changes to the dimensions, which are now recognised by IRB Law 2 to be:

The ball must be oval and consist of
four leather or suitable synthetic panels
Length: 280-300 millimetres
Circumference (end on end): 740-770 millimetres
Circumference (around the middle):
580-620 millimetres
Weight: 410-460 grams
Air pressure: 0.67-0.7 kilograms
per square centimetre

The balls used up until the 1980s were still prone to water damage, despite the use of cod oil and tallow to protect them, and were replaced by the high-tech modern ball. Made out of polyurethane, synthetic leather, laminated polyester, latex and glue, they are now designed to resist the elements and retain their shape.

"And Brian Moore there, praying that this penalty goes over.
'Please give me just this one goal kick and I'll be a good boy
for the rest of the week', he says"
Bill McLaren

RUGBY UNION TIMELINE

1897: Jerseys numbered.

1900: Rugby played at the Paris Olympics.

1903: New Zealand unveil a 2-3-2 formation in the scrum. Ranfurly Shield presented to Auckland.

1905: The New Zealand team become known as the All Blacks.

1906: Forward passes permitted in the US—American Football is born.

1908: Australian touring side nick-named the 'Rabbits' after the pest had been introduced there. A number of letters to English newspapers suggest a better name and 'Wallabies' wins by a few votes. They win the Olympic gold medal.

1910: First Twickenham international.

1913: Women officially allowed to play.

1914-18: More than 100 international players are killed during the war.

1920: USA win Olympic gold.

1924: USA successfully defend their title. A home nations side touring South Africa becomes known as the 'Lions' after the emblem on their ties.

1925: Kiwi Cyril Brownlie becomes the first man sent off in an international match.

1926: First organised sevens tournament held in aid of Middlesex Hospital.

1927: Teddy Wakelam provides live radio commentary for the first time on a British sports event, the England-Wales encounter at Twickenham. Together with the BBC he decides to divide the field into eight squares so that listeners can follow the action across the pitch, hence the origin of the phrase: 'Back to square one'.

1930: IRB takes responsibility for law changes.

1938: The Calcutta Cup match becomes the first international shown on live television.

1939-45: Another 100 internationals are killed in action.

1959: Webb Ellis's grave found by Ross McWhirter from the Guinness Book of Records.

1968: President George W Bush plays for Yale.

1971: Scotland appoint their first coach.

1983: The Women's Rugby Football Union founded by 12 teams.

1985: South Africa cast the deciding vote in favour of a World Cup competition. Australian entrepreneur David Lord pushes for payments to players—the dawn of the professional era.

1987: First World Cup held in Australia and New Zealand. New Zealand beat France in the final.

1991: First—though unofficial—Women's Rugby World Cup held in Cardiff. USA Eagles beat England in the final.

1995: Increased media attention, greater training requirements and player power forces the IRB to allow payments to players. Rugby Union embraces full professionalism. Phillippe Sella becomes the first man to play 100 international matches.

1998: First official Women's World Cup held in Amsterdam. New Zealand beat the USA in the final.

1999: Rugby played in more than 100 countries worldwide, though it has been exported primarily by way of the Commonwealth.

2001: Celtic League rugby introduced.

2003: England become the first northern hemisphere side to win the World Cup. Prop Jason Leonard becomes the most capped player of all-time.

2005: Australian captain George Gregan overtakes Leonard as the world's most capped player. **2006**: France take the Six Nations title though Scotland deny them a Grand Slam. Wales Grand Slam winning coach from 2005, Mike Ruddock, is axed amid rumours that the players revolted and forced him out. New Zealand win the Melbourne Commonwealth Games gold medal for rugby sevens for the third time in succession, narrowly beating England in the final (29-21).

*"From the waist down he has the biggest
legs I've ever seen"*
John Madden

*"Just so that you know, we're signing
Jonah Lomu, not Joanna Lumley, as some
people have reported"*
Cardiff Blues Chairman

INTERNATIONAL RUGBY UNION

——— THE RUGBY WORLD CUP ———

The idea for a Rugby World Cup was first suggested in 1979, but nothing concrete came from the proposal and it wasn't until 1983 that Australia and New Zealand—totally independently as it happened—submitted requests to host the first event, Australia wanting the tournament to coincide with its Bicentenary in 1988, and New Zealand hoping for an event a year earlier. Both bids were turned down by the International Rugby Football Board (IR(f)B) however. Once they were aware of each other's interest, the two nations joined forces, conducted a feasibility study and settled on 1987 to avoid clashes with the Olympic Games and the FIFA World Cup. In March 1985 the eight IRB members—Australia, New Zealand, South Africa, France, England, Scotland, Ireland and Wales—voted in favour of the competition by six votes to two. Ireland and Scotland felt the competition threatened their amateur status, while France, though pro the tournament, wanted more nations to be invited. South Africa would not be invited at all as the country was still suffering the international sports boycott.

The Rugby World Cup was first held in Australia and New Zealand in 1987. Now the third largest sporting event in the world, it is held every four years, with teams competing for the prestigious Webb Ellis Trophy.

THE RUGBY WORLD CUP AT A GLANCE

YEAR	HOST COUNTRY	WINNERS	LOSING FINALISTS	SCORE
1987	New Zealand/Australia	New Zealand	France	29-9
1991	England	Australia	England	12-6
1995	South Africa	South Africa	New Zealand	15-12
1999	Wales	Australia	France	35-12
2003	Australia	England	Australia	20-17
2007	France			
2011	New Zealand			

THE SIX NATIONS
CHAMPIONSHIP

This was originally called the Home Championship when
contested by England, Ireland, Scotland and Wales, then,
with the addition of France in 1910, the Five Nations,
and finally, the Six Nations when Italy joined in 2000.
With the first international matches being played between
the home nations from 1871 onwards, it was only a
matter of time before a championship was devised. The
first was played in 1883, with England winning.

The teams play each other once, usually in February and
March, with home advantage alternating year on year.
Two points are awarded for a win, one for a draw and
none for a loss. The team with the most points after their
five matches is declared the Six Nations champions. If a
team wins all five matches, it is said to have completed a

CAPTAIN	HEAD COACH	TICKETS SOLD	TV AUDIENCE
David Kirk	Brian Lochore	600,000	300 million
Nick Farr-Jones	Bob Dwyer	1 million	1.75 billion
Francois Pienaar	Kitch Christie	1 million	2.67 billion
John Eales	Rod Macqueen	1.75 million	3 billion
Martin Johnson	Clive Woodward	1.84 million	3.5 billion

'Grand Slam', and a team that either finishes bottom of the table or wins no matches is said to have 'won' the 'Wooden Spoon'.

If one of the original four home nations beats the other three in any given year, they are said to have completed a Triple Crown, while the winners of the England-Scotland match are presented with the Calcutta Cup. Since 2000 the winner of the England-Ireland match has been presented with the Millennium Trophy.

France was briefly expelled from the tournament in 1930 amid accusations of payments to players and uncontrollable on-field violence. They were readmitted for the 1940 season but the Second World War precluded their participation until 1947.

SIX NATIONS CHAMPIONSHIP WINNERS

TEAM	HOME VENUE	ENTRIES	OUTRIGHT WINS
England	Twickenham	106	25
Wales	Millennium Stadium★	106	23
Scotland	Murrayfield	106	14
Ireland	Landsdowne Road	106	10
France	Stade de France★	76	15
Italy	Stadio Flaminio	7	0

★Until 1997 Wales played at the Cardiff Arms Park. While the new stadium was being built they played their home games

TRI-NATIONS WINNERS

TEAM	PLAYED	WON	DRAWN	LOST
New Zealand	40	27	0	13
Australia	40	16	1	23
South Africa	40	16	1	23

SHARED WINS	TRIPLE CROWNS	GRAND SLAMS	GRAND SLAM YEARS
10	23	14	1913,1914,1921,1923, 1924,1928,1934,1937, 1957,1980,1991,1992 1995,2003
11	18	9	1908,1909,1911,1950, 1952,1971,1976,1978, 2005
8	10	3	1925,1984,1990
8	8	1	1948
8	-	8	1968,1977,1981,1987, 1997,1998,2002,2004
0	-	0	

embley. Until 1998 France played at the Parc des Princes.

BONUS POINTS	OVERALL POINTS	CHAMPIONS
19	127	1996,1997,1999 2002,2003,2005
21	87	2000,2001
15	81	1998,2004

THE TRI-NATIONS

This tournament, organised by SANZAR, a consortium of rugby governing bodies, is the southern counterpart to the Six Nations, and is contested by South Africa, New Zealand and Australia. It is a relatively new competition (1996) and was designed to promote southern hemisphere rugby in the professional era. The sides play each other twice, usually in July and August, on a home and away basis, with the games between Australia and New Zealand doubling as Bledisloe Cup matches.

The points system differs from that used in the Six Nations. Four points are awarded for a win, two for a draw and none for a loss. A bonus point is awarded if a team scores four or more tries, or by the team that loses if it does to by less than seven points.

THE BRITISH AND IRISH LIONS

It didn't take long for the game of rugby to spread from public school playing fields to the Commonwealth countries. By 1888 a representative side from the four home unions decided to tour Australia and New Zealand, though the move was not sanctioned by the RFU and no Test matches were played. The 22 players who travelled played 53 matches, 35 under rugby union laws – of which they won 27 – and 18 under Australian Rules – of which they won just six.

In 1891 a side backed by Cecil Rhodes toured South Africa. It won all three Tests and every provincial game, the first, and so far only, side to remain unbeaten. By the time of the next tour to the continent (1896), the home nations had been weakened by the loss of players to the new rugby league and the side was exclusively made up of English- and Irishmen. South Africa rallied to win the last Test match wearing their lucky green Old Diocesan shirts.

Though the side toured Australia in 1899, winning three of the four matches, the game there began to decline. Its popularity was eroded from within by the rise of both rugby league and Australian Rules, both offshoots from the union game. Thankfully, teams from New Zealand and South Africa stepped in to fill the void. The 1903 tourists were the first to lose a Test series in South Africa, then they succumbed to the mighty All Blacks in both 1904 and 1908. Southern hemisphere rugby was stealing the north's thunder. The 1910 tour to South Africa was the first to officially represent the four home unions, but they couldn't contain the Springboks and lost two of the three Tests.

After the Great War the tourists visited South Africa. The 1924 team were the first to be known as Lions, by virtue of the emblem on their ties, but the home side again proved too strong and the tourists lost all three Tests. They didn't fare much better in New Zealand in 1930, winning just one of the four Tests, but the trip did establish their playing colours: red shirts, white shorts, and blue socks with green trim represented the four home unions.

The side wouldn't win a series in New Zealand until 1971, with much of the same team winning again on the infamous tour of South Africa three years later. The Lions were put under pressure not to go as the country was struggling with its apartheid regime and protesters gathered at every hotel, but there was an incentive there for the players: no touring side, including the great New Zealanders, had ever beaten the Springboks at home. Irish legend Willie John McBride recalled another obstacle the tourists faced:

"You know you're up against it when the ref shouts 'our ball' at the put-in to the scrum"

Having voiced his concerns over the standards set by referees, as well as the blatant violence from the Springboks towards his own team, McBride introduced the most famous call in rugby history: the '99'. At the sound of the words 'ninety-nine' every Lion would stop what they were doing and belt the nearest South African player. He claimed there was method in this madness as too many of his players were being singled out for punishment. At the call there would be thirty seconds of violence and then the match would continue. The referee couldn't send all the players from the field and the South Africans couldn't keep interrupting play by scrapping. It was an unsatisfactory medium but it worked and the Lions won the series.

The early 1980s saw the Lions struggle on difficult tours to South Africa and New Zealand. Finlay Calder's 1989 team finally registered a series win, against Australia, when David Campese gifted the tourists victory while attempting a breakout move from behind his own goal line. The '90s started off badly with Gavin Hastings' team narrowly losing out in New Zealand, and then it was the turn of England's Martin Johnson to lead the first professional tourists to South Africa in 1997. It was a tough ask; South Africa were the reigning world champions and were rightly acknowledged as the finest team in world rugby.

Despite this, the Lions emerged victorious, winning the series 2-1 after what was a hugely successful tour.

Johnson became the first man to captain two tours when he stepped into the breach for the 2001 trip to Australia, the then world champions. The Lions roared in Brisbane and ran out comfortable victors 29-13 but the hosts fought back to win the next two Tests, the third by the narrowest of margins. Though the defeat was a massive disappointment, the Lions had again silenced the doubters who predicted their demise in the professional era. The 2005 trip to New Zealand was unsuccessful. The hosts were too strong in every department and took the series 3-0.

THE CUPS

The Calcutta Cup

The Calcutta Football Club in India was disbanded in 1877. The club's remaining rupees were melted down into the Calcutta Cup, which was then presented to the RFU. The cup itself has three rearing snake handles and an elephant on top, and was to be awarded to the winner of the annual England-Scotland match. (The first was played in 1871, making it the oldest international fixture.) England didn't win the cup until 1880.

The Bledisloe Cup

Lord Bledisloe, Governor-General of New Zealand, donated this enormous silver cup in 1931. It is contested annually by Australia and the All Blacks. A world record crowd of 109,874 watched the 2000 Bledisloe Cup match in Sydney.

The Webb Ellis Trophy

The cup, a copy of goldsmith Paul de Lamerie's 1740 trophy, was made by Garrard's in 1906, and was chosen as the Rugby World Cup in 1985. It is made from silver gilt and stands 38 centimetres tall. It has two scroll handles, one featuring a satyr and the other a nymph. Chairman of the Rugby World Cup John Kendall-Carpenter (England), Air Commodore Bob Weighill (England), Ronnie Dawson (Ireland), Keith Rowlands (Wales), Bob Stuart and Dick Littlejohn (New Zealand), and Australians Nick Shehadie and Ross Turnbull approved of the trophy being called the World Cup and decided unanimously on its name. It was first presented to New Zealand's David Kirk at Eden Park, Auckland, after his side's victory over France in the 1987 final.

The Trophee des Bicentennaires

The cup is a bronze statue featuring two players in a tackle. It was donated by the French Rugby Union to Australia in 1988—and first contested on an annual, home and away basis in 1989—to coincide with the bicentenaries of the two countries.

The Six Nations Trophy

Silversmith James Brent-Ward designed this trophy, first presented to France as Five Nations champions in 1993. It is made from 200 ounces (six kilograms) of sterling silver, though champagne damage to the inside means it now has a gold plated lining. It has 15 sides (one for each player) and three handles (one for each official), and the finial on the lid is interchangeable depending on which nation holds the trophy.

"He'll have had a couple of stitches in his right lip"
Tim Horan

The Cook Cup

The cup, designed by Royal Doulton in London, is made from crystal and was established in 1997. It is contested on a home and away basis by Australia and England, and was named after the seafaring hero who mapped much of the Australian coastline.

The Hopetoun Cup

This trophy was established in 1998 and is contested by Australia and Scotland. It was also designed by Royal Doulton and is made from crystal. A Scotsman, the seventh Earl of Hopetoun was Governor-General of Australia in 1901.

The Landsdowne Cup

This cup was donated by the club in Sydney of the same name—which was named after the ground in Dublin—and has been contested by Australia and Ireland since 1999. It is made from Irish Waterford crystal.

The Mandela Plate

Nelson Mandela addressed the crowd in Melbourne in 2000 at the world's first indoor Test match. He announced the inaugural competition for the plate, to be held between South Africa and Australia within the Tri-Nations series.

The Puma Trophy

This was established as a perpetual trophy between Argentina and Australia. The two sides first contested a match in 1979 but have met as recently as the opening game of the 2003 Rugby World Cup.

Tom Richards Trophy

This crystal trophy has the face of the only Australian to become a Lion etched into it. Tom Richards toured England with Australia in 1908, and later played for Gloucester—making him eligible for the Lions. The side toured South Africa in 1910 and when one of the players was injured, Richards, who was living in South Africa at the time, was called up as a replacement. The trophy is now awarded to the victors of the Australia and British Lions series and was first contested in 2001.

The Freedom Cup

This trophy, introduced in 2004, is contested every two years by New Zealand and South Africa during the annual Tri-Nations tournament. It was introduced to celebrate the rising number of black players in South African provincial rugby.

The Gallaher Cup

France and New Zealand compete for this cup, named in honour of Irish-born Kiwi legend Dave Gallaher and introduced in 2000. Gallaher himself starred in the 38-8 demolition of the French in 1906. He is buried in Belgium.

The Millennium Trophy

England and Ireland contest this trophy, which was introduced in 2000. It was actually donated to the city of Dublin by Digital in 1988, and is shaped like a horned Viking helmet.

"Every Australian player dreams of playing at Wembley because of the atmosphere and the stigma"
Mark Ella

RUGBY SEVENS

A number of changes were made to the laws of rugby in 1995 so that the sevens game could prosper. Teams consist of seven on-field players (three forwards and four backs) and five rolling substitutes who may be used at any time during the match itself. As the pitch retains the same dimensions as used in the 15-a-side game, the halves are usually seven minutes for preliminary matches and then ten minutes for finals. Conversions must be taken using a drop kick – with the opposition retiring to the halfway line to form up for the restart (taken by the team scoring – another difference) – as must penalties. New Zealand made it three in a row when they retained their status as Commonwealth Games champions in Melbourne in 2006 having won in Kuala Lumpur in 1998 and Manchester in 2002.

The game remains immensely popular. The traditional annual Hong Kong event has been included as part of an International Rugby Board World Series, with teams travelling from Dubai to New Zealand, Hong Kong to Singapore and Paris to London in the eight round series. Points are awarded for winning and placing in each tournament. As the 2006 Hong Kong Sevens approaches, Fiji, captained by the incomparable genius Waisale Serevi, lead England, South Africa and New Zealand. Serevi made his debut at the Hong Kong Sevens in 1989, and though he now claims to be 36, his true age is not known. In his sevens career he has won five Hong Kong titles, two Commonwealth Games silver medals, a World Games gold medal and has scored more points than anyone else in RWC Sevens history.

Few outside New Zealand had heard of Jonah Lomu until he crashed onto the sevens stage in Hong Kong in 1994

International teams all have their nicknames or logo

COUNTRY	NICKNAME/EMBLEM
America	The Eagles
Argentina	Los Pumas
Australia	The Wallabies
Canada	The Canucks
England	Emblem is the Red Rose
Fiji	FMF Flying Fijians
France	Les Bleus *or* Les Coqs
Ireland	Emblem is the Four Leaf Clover
Italy	The Azzurri
Japan	The Cherry Blossoms
New Zealand	The All Blacks
Romania	The Oaks
Samoa	Manu Samoa
Scotland	Emblem is the Thistle or the Bluebell
South Africa	The Springboks
Tonga	'Ikale Tahi
Wales	Emblem is the Prince's Crown with Ostrich feathers

and helped the Kiwis demolish Australia 31-12 in the final.

The first RWC Sevens tournament for the Melrose Cup was held in Edinburgh in 1993, with England emerging as surprise winners. Their team, consisting of the likes of Lawrence Dallaglio, Matt Dawson, Chris Sheasby, Tim

s well as their official and unofficial anthems:

NATIONAL ANTHEM	UNOFFICIAL SONG
The Star Spangled Banner	
Republica Argentina	
Advance Australia Fair	Waltzing Mathilda
O Canada	
God Save the Queen	Swing Low, Sweet Chariot
God Save the Queen (May	The Cibi
God bless Fiji forever more)	
La Marseillaise	
The Soldier's Song (Amhran	Ireland's Call
na Bhfiann)	
Republicana Italiana	Inno di Mameli
The Emperor's Reign	
God Defend New Zealand	The Haka
Wake up Romania	
The Banner of Freedom	
God Save the Queen	Flower of Scotland
Nkosi Sikelel' iAfrika	
Pule'anga Tonga	
Land of my Fathers	Bread of Heaven
(Hen Wlad fy Nhadau)	

Rodber and Andrew Harriman, beat Fiji in the semi-finals and a Micheal Lynagh and David Campese strengthened Australia 21-17 in the final.

A Serevi inspired Fiji won in 1997 and had the honour of having themselves immortalised by a proud nation in a set of 50 cent- and dollar stamps.

BIZARRE RUGBY MOMENTS

London Wasps sent their representative to the wrong
address on the day they were due to help found the RFU
in 1871. Another version of events has the man so drunk
that he couldn't find the restaurant in the first place!

During the Portsmouth Victoria versus Southampton
Trojans match in 1886 the ball rebounded off a stray dog
and the Victorians touched down as a result. The referee
awarded the try as the dog was not classed as a spectator,
which would have nullified the score.

Andrew Stoddart (the last man to captain England at both
rugby and cricket) seemed certain to score for his country
against the touring Maori side in 1889 when Tom Ellison's
last ditch tackle tore his shorts metres from the line. As the
players formed a guard around Stoddart to wait for a new
pair, the referee, Rowland Hill (then secretary of the
RFU), mistakenly allowed play to continue and Frank
Evershed picked up the loose ball and strolled in for an
easy try. The tourists were so disgusted that three walked
off in protest, while Hill again allowed the game to continue. Amazingly the incident was blamed on the Maoris
and they were forced to write a letter of apology to the
RFU, and its secretary, the text of which was dictated by
Hill himself!

The Corinthians soccer club challenged the Barbarians to
a sports festival in 1892. Thanks largely to the efforts of
C.B. Fry the footballers won the athletics section, then
took the football match 6-0 despite the rugby players

using the hand-off to dispatch their opponents. Incredibly they also won the rugby fixture 14-12, beating a largely English pack that had just completed a Triple Crown without conceding a score. The Barbarians salvaged something from the contest, taking the cricket match by four wickets, the incomparable Fry falling for just 25 runs.

England flanker Leo Price caught the ball from the kick-off in the 1923 clash against Wales. With the defence closing in he tried a dropped goal, but the effort was so awful that it went straight up and down. The Welsh were so bamboozled by the tactic, however, that they couldn't stop Price re-gathering the ball and scoring a try.

England wing Carston Catcheside high-jumped over the six-foot French fullback Laurent Pardo to score a famous try at Twickenham in 1924. But the French were quick learners. Their wing Jacques Ballarin cleared England's Bev Chantrill for a try later in the same match. King George V was not as impressed, labelling the tactic dangerous for both players. In fact, back in 1899 Kiwi Barney Armit died when he landed on his head trying the same move.

Bristol's Sam Tucker was inexplicably dropped for the England-Wales championship match in January 1930, but when his replacement injured a toe at the last minute, selectors drafted him back into the side with a phone call at 12.25 pm on match day. Tucker packed his kit and raced to Filton Aerodrome, boarding a two-seater bi-plane with open cockpit at 1.50. On landing in Cardiff barely twenty minutes later, Tucker hitched to the ground, talked his way through a police cordon and joined his team with five minutes to spare.

In the first televised international match England's Hal Sever only had to touch the ball down to win the 1938 Calcutta Cup when desperate Scottish defence forced him to collide with the goal post and drop the ball. It was collected by the Scots who launched a counter-attack that put Wilson Shaw in for the winning try at the other end.

When respected touch judge George Riches intervened to break up a brawl in the Royal Naval Engineering College-Camborne match in 1967, the referee mistakenly thought he was attacking the College men and sent him off!

After the England versus France game in 1982, the English players were each given a bottle of aftershave at the post-match banquet. Maurice Colclough secretly drained his into a plant pot and refilled it with white wine, then challenged the team to a drinking contest. Prop Colin ('not so') Smart took up the challenge and was immediately taken to hospital!

Referee George Crawford became so fed up with the fighting between Bristol and Newport players in 1985 that he left the field, showered, and drove off. A local fireman answered the call and officiated for the remainder of the match.

A number of spectators were injured when the groundsman's shed, on which they were perched to watch a Ranfurly Shield match at Masterton in 1927, collapsed. Hawke's Bay thought they'd beaten rivals Wairarapa 21-10 in the match itself, and thereby regained the Log O'Wood, but they'd fielded an ineligible player and were stripped of the title.

Angry about a stiff arm tackle that had laid out South Canterbury's Eddie Smith in their 1961 match against the touring French, a woman spectator ran onto the pitch and clouted French captain Michel Crauste round the back of the head!

Brothers Don and Ian Clarke faced each other at the Arms Park in 1964. Don was playing for the touring All Blacks while Ian was selected for the Barbarians in the traditional season finale. Midway through the first half Don sent a 25 drop out straight to his brother, who shocked everyone by calling for a mark and then taking a pot at goal. The prop had never kicked a goal of any importance in his career but he managed to score three points to the amazement of team mates on both sides!

During the final Test between New Zealand and South Africa in 1981, a light aircraft dropped flour bombs onto the pitch at Eden Park, Auckland. Even though one laid out Kiwi Gary Knight, his side won the series 2-1.

Fullback George Nepia was refereeing a charity match when the ball bounced up in front of him. Unable to resist, the ex-player gathered it and ran it under the posts!

THE BARBARIANS

William Percy Carpmael, an outstanding player for both Blackheath and Cambridge University, is credited with forming the Barbarians. (The name supposedly comes from the defeat of Varius by the barbarian Arminius in Germany nearly 2000 years ago.) Carpmael was disappointed by the amount of rugby being played in the off-season and decided to put together an invitation side for the very best players in the country. The only qualifications he considered when assembling the team were that their standard of rugby was sufficiently high and that the player should conduct himself suitably on and off the field. There would be no discrimination whatsoever, regardless of race, colour or creed. On December 27, 1890, his Barbarians team took the field against Hartlepool and promptly won their first match 9-4.

As their popularity grew, the Barbarians gained worldwide respect for their flair, courage, spirit and passion, but above all for their sense of fair play. On January 31, 1948, the home unions requested a match between the Barbarians and the touring Australian side so they could raise money for the visitors to travel home via Canada. It was played at Cardiff Arms Park in front of 45,000 fans and was so successful that any touring southern hemisphere side thereafter was scheduled to play the Barbarians in their last match, the so-called 'Final Challenge'. The Baa-Baas won this one 9-6.

"Barbarian rugby is all about a feeling, spirit, essence or soul to the game"
Sir Wilson Whineray, Barbarian and All Black

"The game against the All Blacks is one I will never forget,
and those of us who played in it will never be allowed to forget"
Gareth Edwards

Here the Welshman was referring to the Barbarians versus
All Blacks match, perhaps the greatest game of all time, in
1973, which his side went on to win 23-11. The match was
just a few minutes old when Edwards rounded off a move
that had been started by Phil Bennett inside his own 25.
The ball passed through eight pairs of hands before
Edwards touched down in the corner. Cliff Morgan's
commentary is as unforgettable as the try itself:

"This is great stuff. Phil Bennett covering. Chased by Alasdair Scown.
Brilliant! Oh, that's brilliant! John Williams. Brian Williams. Pullin.
John Dawes, great dummy. David, Tom David. The half-way line.
Brilliant by Quinnell! This is Gareth Edwards! A dramatic start!
What a score!"

Membership is still by invitation only, and the club is also
unique in that it has no ground, no clubhouse, no entry fee,
no subscription and plays no home matches. It is a touring
club in every sense. The jersey is black and white, the
shorts are black and the players' socks must be those of his
usual club.

The side rarely accepts an invitation to a sevens tournament, but when it does, there have been spectacular results.
The Barbarians are the only European side to win the prestigious Hong Kong Sevens and have won the Middlesex
Sevens on each of the three times they've entered (1934,
1997, 1998).

CLUB RUGBY UNION

── THE PREMIERSHIP ──

Before 1987 there were only friendly matches and the regional cup competitions played in domestic English rugby. Then the 108 Courage Leagues were formed from over a thousand clubs across the country, each with its own rules for promotion and relegation. During its first ten years Bath and Leicester dominated the league, Wasps being the only club to break their monopoly on the title.

As the sport toyed with the idea of professionalism, a new sponsor for the top flight was found, and Allied Dunbar put their name to the League between 1997 and 2000. This was an era dominated by the Leicester Tigers. They claimed four consecutive titles and amassed 52 straight home wins. Some clubs, notably Richmond and London Scottish, struggled to find financial backing in the first years of professional rugby and were forced into administration. Others, like Northampton and Newcastle, were fortunate in that they attracted wealthy benefactors, and they thrived.

Zurich took over from Allied Dunbar in 2000 and remained as the main sponsor until 2006 when Guinness put its name to the Premiership. The twelve teams in the top league play each other home and away to battle it out for the right to play in the Premiership Final at Twickenham, the league leaders playing the winners of a second and third place play-off. London Wasps' director of Rugby, Warren Gatland, guided his team to three successive victories from 2003 to 2005.

The Powergen Cup

This is the national knockout trophy contested by 132 rugby clubs nationwide. It was first played in 1972 and has grown through a variety of sponsors including John Player, Pilkington and Tetley's Bitter. It remains the premier domestic cup competition, with the final being played at Twickenham in front of capacity crowds.

The Heineken European Cup

Launched in 1995, and consisting of twelve teams from Ireland, France, Wales, Italy and Romania, the first European Cup ran for just fifteen matches, the four pool winners advancing directly to the semi-finals. 21,800 then watched Toulouse beat Cardiff 21-18 in extra time at the Arms Park. The following year the competition was expanded to include teams from England and Scotland, and the year after that teams played each other on a home and away basis. In all 70 matches were played and spectator numbers increased dramatically.

In the 1999/2000 season four different nationalities contested the semi-finals, with Northampton ending over a hundred years' wait for a trophy when they beat Munster 9-8 in front of nearly 70,000 at Twickenham.

"That's what this team is all about: pace, speed and quickness"
Steve Black

The Bowring Bowl/MMC Trophy

This cup is contested by Oxford and Cambridge Universities. The Varsity (a British abbreviation of the word university) Match was first held in 1872 at 'The Parks' ground in Oxford, and was won by the home side. The return match the following year was played at 'Parkers Piece', Cambridge, but from then on it was decided to move the fixture to a neutral venue, the first being the Kennington Oval in Surrey. In 1887 the match was moved to the Queen's Club, where it stayed until 1921 when it was switched to Twickenham. Cambridge have won 58 fixtures, Oxford 52, and there have been 14 draws. Previous players have included Gavin Hastings, Rob Andrew, Simon Danielli, Kevin Tkachuk, David Humphrys and Stuart Barnes.

The Ranfurly Shield

In 1901 the Earl of Ranfurly donated the shield to the NZRFU, but left it up to the union as to what form the competition should take. The NZRFU decided that the first winner should be the side with the best record in 1902 and thereafter it would be contested on a challenge basis, with one of the unions attempting to wrest the 'Log of Wood', as it became known, from the holders. Auckland remained unbeaten in 1902 and were the inaugural winners.

The Super 14

Initially called the South Pacific Championship, this tournament was launched in 1986, with three teams from New Zealand, two from Australia, and the Fijian national side. Australia went on to win the 1991 World Cup and the upsurge in interest forced organisers to re-launch the competition as a Super Six in 1992. The standard was high, and the interest level maintained, so the following

EUROPEAN CUP FINALS

YEAR	VENUE	WINNERS
1996	Cardiff Arms Park	Toulouse
1997	Cardiff Arms Park	Brive
1998	Stade Lescure	Bath
1999	Landsdowne Road	Ulster
2000	Twickenham	Northampton
2001	Parc des Princes	Leicester
2002	Millennium Stadium	Leicester
2003	Lansdowne Road	Toulouse
2004	Twickenham	Wasps
2005	Murrayfield	Toulouse
2006	Millenium Stadium	Munster
2007		

year the tournament was expanded to ten teams, including provincial sides from South Africa, and Western Samoa. In 1996 it was upgraded to include two more teams – becoming the Super 12 – and in 2006 another two (Australia's Western Force and South Africa's Central Cheetahs) were added. At the beginning of the 2006 season, there were five teams from New Zealand and South Africa, and four from Australia. Bonus points are awarded to teams scoring more than four tries per match and the emphasis is always on fast, attacking rugby.

"There's no such thing as a lack of confidence.
You either have it or you don't"
Rob Andrew

"They've got old shoulders on their heads"
JPR Williams

RUNNERS UP	SCORE
Cardiff	21-18
Leicester	28-9
Brive	19-18
Colomiers	21-6
Munster	9-8
Stade Francais	34-30
Munster	15-9
Perpignan	22-17
Toulouse	27-20
Stade Francais	18-12
Biarritz	23-19

SUPER 14 WINNERS

1986	Canterbury	1997	Auckland
1987	Canterbury/Auckland	1998	Canterbury
1988	Auckland	1999	Canterbury
1989	Auckland	2000	Canterbury
1990	Auckland	2001	ACT Brumbies
1991	Not held	2002	Canterbury
1992	Queensland (Super Six)	2003	Auckland
1993	Transvaal (Super Ten)	2004	ACT Brumbies
1994	Queensland	2005	Canterbury
1995	Queensland	2006	Canterbury
1996	Auckland (Super 12)	2007	

—— FASCINATING RUGBY FACTS ——

According to Maori mythology Tane-rore, son of the Sun God Tam-nui-to-ra and his wife Hine-raumati, performed the first haka. The All Blacks' derivative, the Ka Mate haka, dates to 1810 when Chief Te Rauparaha of the Ngati Toa tribe hid from his enemy in a food storage pit. When he tried to escape, he found a man standing over him, but instead of killing him, the man turned out to be another chief from a friendly tribe. So overjoyed was he at his good fortune that Te Rauparaha performed a haka with the words:

> *It is death, it is death. It is life, it is life.*
> *It is death, it is death. It is life, it is life.*
> *This is the hairy man who fetched the sun*
> *And caused it to shine again.*
> *One upward step, another upward step.*
> *An upward step, another!*
> *The sun shines!*

The 1905 *Originals* were the first touring side to begin a match will this challenge. In August 2005 the All Blacks unveiled a new haka – *Kapa O Pango*. The translation complements the game and the history more than the original but it will only be used on special occasions:

> *Let me become one with the land,*
> *This is our land that rumbles,*
> *And it's my time! It's my moment!*
> *This defines us as the All Blacks,*
> *It's my time! It's my moment!*
> *Our dominance, our supremacy will triumph,*
> *And will be placed on high,*
> *Silver fern!*
> *All Blacks!*
> *Silver fern!*
> *All Blacks!*

In 1888 a New Zealand Natives team toured Great Britain. They played 107 matches over a period of 13 months!

When the Football Association fell in favour of codifying their game to the Eton Rules in 1863, Blackheath walked out and founded the RFU. The clause that proved to be the stumbling block between the two sides outlawed players hacking each others' shins, except those of the man with the ball!

James Gilbert, nephew of the famous maker of rugby balls, William, was so powerfully built that he used to inflate the match balls on lung power alone!

James Marsh played two caps for Scotland in 1889 before settling in Manchester. His football skills caught the eyes of the English selectors in 1892 and he was awarded a cap for that season's England-Ireland clash.

An English poll conducted in September 2005 showed that 2/3 of those asked didn't believe the Webb Ellis story. In a similar vote, Jonny Wilkinson's drop goal to win the 2003 world cup was listed as the third most newsworthy sporting event in the last 50 years. It was beaten only by Torvill and Dean's perfect 6s at the Sarajevo winter Olympics in 1984 and Bobby Moore lifting the football world cup in 1966.

It is said that Baron Pierre de Coubertin founded the Olympic Games having been inspired by the virtues of rugby played in Britain in the last decades of the 19th century.

Os Du Randt, a 21 stone South African prop, tried to tackle Welsh Lions centre Scott Gibbs on the 1997 tour, but only managed to floor himself. A doctor described the collision as like being in a car crash and the nick-name has stuck with Gibbs ever since.

Kiwi Jeff Wilson played international cricket before becoming an All Black.

As a member of Richmond's King's House school choir, England's Lawrence Dallaglio sang backing vocals for Tina Turner on *We don't need another hero* in 1985. Unbeknownst to the player, he was owed a royalty payment of £250, which he finally received in October 2005.

According to Billy Wallace, a member of *The Originals* (the first New Zealand team to tour Great Britain in 1905/6), the name *All Blacks* originated because of an article in a London newspaper describing them as *all backs*, due to their speed and angles of running. So, although they wore a black kit, it seems likely that they got their name as a result of some confusion over a missing letter!

Russian Prince Alexander Obolensky fled his homeland for England in 1917. He was granted British citizenship and was called into the England squad in 1936. His 17 tries in four matches tipped him for greatness, but he was killed when his Hurricane fighter crashed near Ipswich in 1940.

Former England captain Will Carling famously described the RFU executives as "57 old farts". He was sacked immediately, only to be reinstated when the players refused to play for anyone else.

World Cup winning South African scrum-half Joost van der Westhuizen made the first big tackle on Kiwi giant Jonah Lomu in the 1995 final, this despite him suffering from two broken ribs.

Despite Argentinean Frederico Mendez' long career he will best be remembered for his punch that felled England's Paul Ackford at Twickenham in 1990. He wrongly believed the lock had stamped on him and decked him with a giant haymaker in retaliation.

It is rumoured that the All Black team was deliberately given food poisoning before their 1995 World Cup Final clash with hosts South Africa. The seemingly invincible Kiwis lost a number of key players to the illness and went down 15-12 in the match. In one of the defining sporting moments of the twentieth century Nelson Mandela, wearing the once hated shirt of the white Springbok captain, presented the trophy to Francois Pienaar under the slogan 'one team, one nation'.

The same whistle has been used to start the opening match of all five Rugby World Cups. The Evans/Freethy whistle bears an inscription saying it was first used by Gil Evans in the Test match between England and New Zealand in 1905, a match the tourists won 15-0. It was also used by Albert Freethy in the 1924 Olympic final, a match where the USA beat hosts France 17-13, the last time the event was held at the Games. The American team, therefore, are the reigning Olympic champions.

Cyril Brownlie became the first man to be sent off in an international when he was dismissed at Twickenham by Albert Freethy (with the same whistle) in 1925. The touring New Zealand side won all of their 32 matches and became known as 'The Invincibles'. The coin used before the 1925 match was also used by Paul Honiss before the Australia-Argentina match at RWC 2003.

Scot Eric Liddell won seven caps before retiring from rugby in 1923. The next year he won the Olympic 400 metres title in Paris and was immortalised in the 1981 film *Chariots of Fire*.

In the 1920s Italian leader Benito Mussolini claimed his country had invented the sport, it being a direct derivative of *feninda* and *harpastum*, two ancient Roman games. In 1927 he gave rugby its own propaganda committee.

In the 2003 Rugby World Cup England fielded 16 players against Samoa for a few seconds. Despite fearing they would be thrown out of the tournament, they were only fined £10,000 and had coach Dave Reddin banned from the touchline.

Namibia conceded 310 points in their four pool matches at the 2003 Rugby World Cup.

Two devoutly religious teams, South Africa and Samoa

joined each other for a communal prayer on the pitch after their 2003 encounter.

England's scrum-half Matt Dawson refuses to play for the Barbarians after an initiation ceremony led to him being whipped with a cactus.

Seven Randall brothers from Llanelli took on seven Williams brothers from Haverfordwest in an ill-tempered sevens challenge match in 1909, the Williams family winning the glorified fight 8-0.

Welshman Jerry Shea became the first player to score a full house (try, conversion, penalty, dropped goal) in international rugby when his side beat England 19-5 in 1920.

Simon Culhane (New Zealand) scored a world record 45 points (20 conversions and 1 try) on his debut, the 145-17 thrashing of Japan at the World Cup in 1995. In the same game Marc Ellis scored a record six tries. England's Charlie Hodgson scored 44 points on his debut against Romania six years later in the 134-0 victory. This winning margin was eclipsed in 2003 as Australia notched up 142 unanswered points against Namibia at the World Cup. It should be mentioned that Hong Kong fullback Ashley Billington scored ten tries (50 points) against Singapore in a World Cup qualifier in 1995. The final score was 164-13! And Kiwi Rod Heeps scored eight tries against Northern New South Wales in 1962.

A one-armed player, Mr Wakeham kicked 13 goals from

13 attempts for Newton Abbot against Plymouth in 1886.

Pope John Paul II represented Poland at rugby!

Five Smith brothers played for New Zealand side Bush against Wairapara in 1903. This feat was equalled by the famous Clarkes of Waikato in 1961. Don and Ian went on to share 55 All Black caps.

Five players have won more than 100 international caps: George Gregan (Australia) has 118, Jason Leonard (England) 114 (plus five Lions appearances), Phillippe Sella (France) 111, Fabien Pelous (France) 108 and David Campese (Australia) 101. Campese is also the world's top Test try scorer with 64. England's Rory Underwood is second with 49.

The average match at RWC 2003 produced 260 passes, 130 rucks and mauls, 60 tactical kicks and 64 points.

When the first All Blacks came to Britain in 1905 they weren't given much hope against the English club sides. They surprised everyone but themselves in their first tour match against county champions Devon, eventually running out 55-4 winners. Local newspaper editors didn't believe the score, assuming there to have been a transmission error, and some even corrected the result for their morning editions. One even acknowledged the strength of the west-countrymen and ran the headline Devon 55, New Zealand 4.

In the 1963 Wales versus Scotland clash at Murrayfield,

the referee counted 111 lineouts, one every 43 seconds. The law was changed shortly afterwards so that the team kicking the ball into touch gave away the throw in instead of retaining it.

Every year more then 200,000 games of rugby union are played worldwide.

Samoan Brian Lima's bone-crunching tackles earned him the nickname *The Chiropractor*!

MORE BIZARRE RUGBY MOMENTS

New Zealand legend Colin Meads reputedly trained by running up and down hills with a sheep under each arm. Indeed his strength and fierce competitiveness on the pitch were renowned (he played on with a broken arm against Eastern Transvaal in 1970). In 1966 Lion David Watkins was taken off on a stretcher after colliding with the Kiwi's knee; in 1967 Meads was sent off at Murrayfield for aiming a boot at the Scottish fly-half; in 1968 he forcibly removed Wallaby Ken Catchpole from a ruck by his leg and ripped his groin irreparably; and in 1969 Welsh hooker Jeff Young broke his jaw on Meads' fist.

In 1986 the French pack found New Zealander Wayne Shelford at the bottom of a ruck and raked him out fiercely, leaving him with a concussion, smashed front teeth and a ripped scrotum. Shelford promptly instructed the physio to stitch him up so he could play on!

Levin Wanderers wing John Tupo was tackled by a spectator seconds before he would have scored the winning try at the end of a district final against Athletic in 2000. The man was arrested but officials decided against awarding a penalty try and the match was drawn 13-13.

In 1891 the Irish fullback Dolway Walkington caught a loose kick against the Welsh at Stradey Park, Llanelli. Then, as he was very short-sighted, he calmly removed his monocle and dropped a perfect goal! It was reported that he would remove the eye piece before every tackle, and that he'd taken it out for a crucial conversion against England in Dublin in 1880, which he then missed.

Irishman Colm Tucker was used to having his name spelt wrongly, but even he was surprised to read that the 'T' had been substituted with an 'F' in the program for the 1980 match against France. As he came on to replace John O'Driscoll after twenty minutes the French announcer duly repeated the mistake.

In the 1999 Five Nations match between Ireland and France, Irish hooker Keith Wood was dumped to the turf during a collapsed scrum. He emerged covered in paint – courtesy of the on-pitch advertising – and played the rest of the game with a blue head!

Ireland's Brian O'Driscoll was penalised for tackling Australian George Smith by the hair in 2003!

Though it's possibly an urban myth, there is a story involving the College of Surgeons of Ireland playing junior level rugby. Unfortunately all names and dates have disappeared from the source material. During the match one of the players dislocated his femur and a number of trainee medics rushed to help the screaming boy. They diagnosed the problem and forced the femur back into the hip joint, though the boy's screaming only intensified. Apparently the femur snagged one of his testicles, which was then crushed as the bone re-entered the socket. The boy ruptured his vocal chords before passing out in agony.

The 1908 England versus Wales game at Bristol was so affected by fog that the Welsh didn't realise they'd left fullback Bert Winfield on the pitch at the end. They were all relaxing in the clubhouse celebrating a 28-19 win by the time someone realised he was missing. Apparently Winfield believed his side had been camped on the England line for the entire second half!

Conditions were so bad during the 1957 Wales-Ireland clash in Cardiff that referee Jack Taylor ordered the entire Welsh team from the field after an hour because their shirts were so black with mud. The clean kit worked wonders and the Welsh went on to win.

Welsh fullback Terry Davies was denied a winning penalty by the goalpost at Twickenham in 1958. Later that night Welsh jockey Fred Mathias and Englishman Brian Attewell broke into the ground and, having failed to remove the offending post, sawed off the crossbar and took it back to Pembrokeshire. They bumped into Davies on the way home and he autographed the bar, then, as the RFU had intervened, and he was a timber merchant, he agreed to replace the crossbar instead of having the original returned!

While warming up for the match against Australia at RWC 2003, Scottish fullback Chris Patterson was knocked out by a high ball that struck him on the temple.

Ed Fry was stripped from the waist down by a Queenslander's tackle in their league clash against New South Wales in 1908, but he still managed to score.

When South African umpire 'Klondike' Raaff appeared to flag compatriot Anton Stegmann into touch in their match against Ireland in Belfast in 1906, the cover defence pulled up and waited for the lineout to form. Unbeknownst to the home team, Raaff was merely celebrating Stegmann's powerful run and the try he then scored was allowed to stand, winning the match for the visitors.

In the Western Province versus Orange Free State match in 1991, lock F.C. Smit was brought to ground by a streaker! Thankfully the commentator resisted the temptation to comment on the quality of the tackle.

South African prop Leon Boshoff took the field for the Golden Cats in 2001 and trampled over the mascot by mistake!

In a 2002 Tri-Nations match between South Africa and New Zealand, a South African fan, Pieter Van Zyl, ran on to the field and attacked referee David McHugh. McHugh had his shoulder dislocated in the confrontation and Van Zyl was charged with assault.

The 1967 Griqualand West-France match at Kimberley was so violent that officials considered introducing a certificate or rating system to decide who was allowed to watch!

In 1911 Frenchman Gaston Vareilles was on his way to play in the home match against Scotland when he jumped off the train to grab a sandwich. By the time he'd paid, the train had left the station and he missed the match, never to play another. Scouting for a last minute replacement in the stadium the French chose spectator Andre Franquenelle. He helped them to their first international victory (16-15) and won another two caps!

In 1969 Frenchman Jean-Pierre Salut ran up a flight of

steps to take his place on the field against Scotland at the Stade Colombes. But he tripped and broke his ankle, thus becoming the only man to be carried from the field without actually making it there in the first place!

Frenchman Lucien Mias led France to a series win in South Africa in 1958 by quaffing a half bottle of rum during the half-time interval!

The French press picked up on the fact that their fly-half for the 1960 season, Pierre Albaladejo, reportedly had flat feet, fallen arches and wore special shoes, and they made a huge issue of the subject. In the Ireland match he kicked three drop goals, two with his left foot and one with his right. Then he pointed out to the press that he'd kicked four drop goals two weeks earlier. In his next international, against Italy the following week, he rubbed their noses in it with another two drops.

In the 2003 Canada versus Tonga match the ball cannoned off a seagull!

When the USA played Japan in 1991, the American anthem was played at half speed!

Irish centre Brian O'Driscoll captained the 2005 Lions in New Zealand, but he lasted only 41 seconds of the first Test before being spear tackled and suffering a broken shoulder.

COMMENTARY CHAOS

"Well, they've got strength in depth and numbers,
but not strength in depth"
Dick Best

"Now, being an Aussie you must be sweating buttocks"
Mark Durden-Smith asks Michael Lynagh for his
thoughts on the game

"I've fantasised about lineouts, even in my sleep sometimes"
Murray Mexted

Grant Nisbett: *"Murray? Murray, can you hear me?"*
Murray Mexted: *"No"*

"Well, what do you think of that? Outstanding!"
"Oh, that is just gorgeous!"
"Oh! Oh! Oh!" "Oh my!"
Murray Mexted and Ian Smith discuss the cheerleaders
without realising they're on air

"And that one has taken Latham in the crotch.
He's got a sharp one right where it hurts"
Chris 'Budda' Handy describes the illegal tackle that sparked
a mass brawl between Australia and South Africa in the
2002 Tri-Nations

"I think the loose forward battle is going to be a classic,
because as you know I've been pumping Marty Leslie for a
couple of years now"
Murray Mexted

"This is going off like a frog in a sock"
Hamish Mackay

"A good punch never hurt anybody"
Rex Mossop

*"There's nothing a tight forward likes more than a loosie
up his backside"*
Murray Mexted

*"I mean we know Matthew Cooper has got tremendous rhythm now.
He's smooth, smooth as a baby's bum. By Jove that didn't slip out,
did it?"*
Grant Nisbett

*"Well, it still does it for me: The tingle up the spine, the
tingle in the loins"*
Murray Mexted

"He's a very good footballer, a constructive falicitator!"
Murray Mexted confuses himself....again

"That's Doddie Weir, leaping like a Scottish salmon"
Bill McLaren

*"Simon Geoghegan is all arms and legs in there.
He looks like a strangled octopus"*
Bill McLaren

"If you put the ball up high enough it can go anywhere"
Steve Smith

*"Well the first half was a half of two halves.
The first half of that half belonged to England while the
second half of the first half belonged to Australia"*
South African commentator

"It's like having three controlled car crashes a week"
England physio Phil Pask

RUGBY LEAGUE

OBJECT OF THE GAME

To win the game a team must score more points than their opposition. The methods of scoring (try, conversion, penalty, dropped goal) are the same as in Rugby Union, as are their execution, but the number of points awarded for each score have evolved separately.

YEAR	TRY	CONVERSION	PENALTY	DROP/FIELD GOAL
Pre-1875	0	2	3	3
1875-1895	1	3	3	3
1895-1897	3	2	3	4
1897-1974	3	2	2	2
1974-1983	3	2	2	1
1983-present	4	2	2	1

The game starts, after the toss of a coin to decide ends and who will kick off, with a place kick in the centre of the field. The team receiving the ball must then use a 'set' of six tackles to move the ball up the field to score. Each time a player is tackled, the count (shouted by the referee) advances by one and a play-the-ball situation arises. If a team uses all their tackles without scoring the ball is handed to their opponents and the tackle count resets. So as not to give the ball away cheaply on the last tackle, it is usual for the attacking side to kick for territory before the handover.

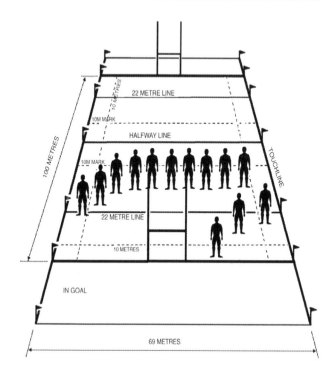

The Line Up

The scrum/forwards: These are typically the big, strong men who take short passes from the dummy-half after the play-the-ball to gain territory by driving up the middle of the pitch in a low-risk strategy. If enough defenders get sucked in to stop these drives, the forwards may look to off-load short passes out of the tackle to maintain possession and gain more ground. Defensively, they try to shore up the middle of the pitch and force opponents into playing wider but riskier moves.

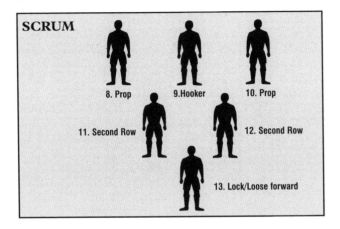

SCRUM

8. Prop 9.Hooker 10. Prop

11. Second Row 12. Second Row

13. Lock/Loose forward

The backs/three-quarters: Usually lighter and faster (as in union), the backs are used creatively in attack, looking for breaks from riskier passes and attempting to confuse defences with tactical kicking. Defensively, the backs must ensure the opposition's quick men can't break through into the open field behind them.

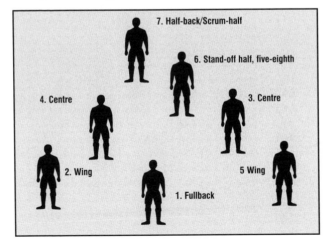

7. Half-back/Scrum-half

6. Stand-off half, five-eighth

4. Centre 3. Centre

2. Wing 5 Wing

1. Fullback

Play-the-Ball

As soon as a player is held in the tackle the remaining defenders must retreat ten metres, with the exception of the tackler and another marker. The player with the ball must then stand, place the ball on the ground and roll it back to his team (most usually the hooker, who is then known as the acting half-back or dummy-half) with the boot. As soon as this has happened, the ball is back in play.

The Scrum

If a side knocks the ball forward, or carries or kicks the ball over the sideline at any time, a scrum is awarded to the defending team. As these are not contested in the modern game, possession for the team putting the ball in is almost guaranteed. If the defending team (without the ball) knocks on, trying to intercept a pass for example, and the ball is re-gathered by the attacking team, the referee will reset the tackle count to zero. These rules appear to overlap those of American Football, with the exception that league players are limited to six tackles, and must therefore gain the most territory possible on each, whereas a new set of four 'downs' is awarded for every ten yards gained in the US.

Penalties

If the referee deems a player to have broken one of the laws he may award a penalty. If this is seen as a serious offence (swinging arm tackle) the player may be sent to the sin-bin (a yellow card and ten minutes off the field) or sent off (red card) for the remainder of the match. The attacking team may choose to try a shot at goal (2 points), have the tackle count reset to give them another set of six, or kick downfield to gain territory while retaining the ball.

The 40/20 kick

This is a new rule to help teams attack and open the game up. Usually when a team forces the ball into touch, the opposition are awarded the resulting scrum. If, however, the kicker is standing between his own forty metre- and goal lines when he kicks, and the ball enters touch on the bounce between his opponents' twenty metre- and goal lines, his team will retain put-in to the scrum.

RUGBY LEAGUE TIMELINE

1886: RFU introduces strictly amateur rules to alienate working-class northern clubs.

1888: RFU pays players to tour Australia.

1892: Clubs in Yorkshire are charged with making payments to players.

1895: Representatives from 21 northern clubs meet at the George Hotel, Huddersfield. They form the Northern Rugby Football Union, which later becomes the Rugby Football League.

1896: Manningham of Bradford win the first NRU championship.

1897: Lineouts abolished. Goals reduced to two points and tries increased to three to make the game more exciting. Batley beat St Helens in the first Challenge Cup Final.

1904: First international match sees England beaten 9-3 by an Other Nationalities team. Northern Union has more members than the RFU.

1906: Northern Union reduces the number of players to 13 and replaces rucks and mauls after a tackle with the play-the-ball.

1907: First league formed. Rules of the game diversify further from union. First touring side (NZ), under Albert Baskerville, visits Britain.

1910: British side tours Australia and New Zealand.

1915: Harold Wagstaff leads Huddersfield to all four domestic cups.

1922: Formation of the Rugby Football League.

1930: French Rugby Union suspended over breaching amateur rules. Many French players turn to the lucrative game of League.

1932: Rugby league first played under floodlights at White City.

1943: First cross-code matches. League armed services sides win both variants.

1949-1950: A record 6.8 million spectators watch at least one league match in Britain.

1951: France defeat Australia in a three Test series and are welcomed home by over 100,000 fans.

1954: First World Cup held in France.

1958: Britain defeat Australia with only eight fit players left on the pitch. Captain Alan Prescott plays for 77 minutes with a broken arm.

1967: Number of tackles limited to four.

1971: Number of tackles increased to six.

1972: Timekeepers and sirens introduced.

1974: Drop goal reduced from two points to one.

1980: First State of Origin match played between Queensland and New South Wales.

1981: First Varsity Match.

1983: Value of a try increased from three to four points. Sin-bin and sixth tackle handover introduced.

1996: First season of Super League. Cross-code matches held at Maine Road, Manchester, and Twickenham, London. Wigan demolish Bath 82-6 under League rules using superior running lines and power, and only go down 44-19 under Union laws. Having only just turned professional, rugby union players have yet to match the skills and fitness of their northern opponents.

1998: Grand Final play-off system introduced.

1999: Last Challenge Cup Final at Wembley.

2000: A record 16 nations contest the World Cup but favourites Australia retain their title.

2001: St Helens win the first Challenge Cup Final held at Twickenham, Union's HQ.

2002: Bradford Bulls win the World Club Championship, defeating Australia's Newcastle Knights 41-26. Russia defeats the USA 54-10 in front of 25,000 in Moscow.

2003: Bradford Bulls become the first team to win the Grand Final and the Challenge Cup in the same year.

2004: Average match attendances for the season reach a new high of 8,570.

2005: The London Broncos are renamed Harlequins. They move to the Twickenham Stoop in west London to ground share with their second division union namesake. Some people predict that this is the first step in unifying the codes, though this seems a long way off yet.

2006: Great Britain manager Philip Clarke steps down after five years in charge.

FOUNDER MEMBERS OF THE NORTHERN RUGBY UNION

(George Hotel, Huddersfield, August 29 1895)

Batley, Bradford, Brighouse Rangers, Broughton Rangers, Dewsbury, Halifax, Huddersfield, Hull, Hunslet, Leeds, Leigh, Liversedge, Manningham, Oldham, Rochdale Hornets, St Helens, Tyldesley, Wakefield Trinity, Warrington, Widnes, Wigan

Stockport were accepted by telephone, while Dewsbury withdrew two days later to be replaced by Runcorn.

INTERNATIONAL RUGBY LEAGUE

THE WORLD CUP

This competition was first held in 1954, but the format has changed repeatedly over the years. There is no set cycle for competition, there being as many as eight and as few as two years between tournaments. Twice in its history the world cup has lasted for over three years!

THE TRI-NATIONS

This is an annual contest held between Great Britain, Australia and New Zealand, to decide the best team in the world. New Zealand and Australia play two home matches before travelling to Britain for the remaining four matches in a round-robin format. The top two teams go on to contest the final.

At the same time as the Tri-Nations, a European Nations Cup and a Pacific Rim Championship are also held, the idea being to improve all teams' chances at the next World Cup.

THE ASHES

The first Australian side to tour the British Isles arrived in

1908. They played three Tests against their hosts and suggested that the series should be called 'The Ashes' (after the cricket), and the name stuck. Since that first tour, Australia have won 20 series and Great Britain (called the Northern Union until 1921, and the Lions or Great Britain thereafter) 19. The southern hemisphere giants have won 13 in a row since 1973.

THE BASKERVILLE SHIELD

This trophy, first contested in 2002, is awarded to the winners of a Test series between Great Britain and New Zealand. It is named after Kiwi Albert Henry Baskerville who organised the tour to the UK in 1907. In fact, the side were the first official international team, and became known as the 'All Golds'. They lost their first ever Test to Wales (8-9), but beat Great Britain in the main series.

THE ANZAC TEST

First played in 1997, this Test match between Australia and New Zealand is scheduled for around ANZAC day. The name for the match was controversial because some claimed it compared the heroic deeds of soldiers in war time to professional players competing for nothing more than bragging rights. Australia have won five of the six matches (no contest between 2001 and 2003), with New Zealand scoring their only win in 1998.

THE VICTORY CUP

Russia, France, Great Britain's Amateur Rugby League Association, and the USA contest this trophy annually. It is run in knock-out fashion, with the two winners of the

WORLD CUP WINNERS

Year	Hosts	Winners
1954	France	Great Britain
1957	Australia	Australia*
1960	England	Great Britain*
1968	Australia/New Zealand	Australia
1970	England	Australia
1972	France	Great Britain
1975	Worldwide	Australia*
1977	Australia/New Zealand	Australia
1985-'88	Worldwide	Australia
1989-'92	Worldwide	Australia
1995	England/Wales	Australia
2000	UK/Ireland/France	Australia
2008	Australia/New Zealand	

*League positions determined the winners. The 1960 match was the last league game, with both teams going in unbeaten, so it proved to be a virtual final.

**The scores were still level after 20 minutes of extra time so

first round meeting in the final. The runners up play a match for the Victory Bowl. Both competitions are designed to promote rugby league abroad, with a view to developing the game globally. From 2003 the tournament was expanded to include more teams.

"And he's got an ice-pack on his groin so it's probably not the old shoulder injury"
Ray French

Runners up	Final Score	Crowd
France	16-12	30,000
Great Britain	No final match	
Australia	10-3	32,733
France	20-2	54,290
Great Britain	12-7	
Australia	10-10**	4,500
England***		
Great Britain	13-12	24,457
New Zealand	25-12	47,363
Great Britain	10-6	73,631
England	16-8	66,540
New Zealand	40-12	44,300

Great Britain were awarded the title by virtue of their better league position.
***In 1975 and 1995 Great Britain was divided up into teams from England and Wales for the benefit of the tournament. In 2000 Scotland and Ireland also provided teams

FASCINATING LEAGUE MOMENTS

In the 1968 World Cup group match between Great Britain and Australia the crowd reached 62,256, which would remain the highest attendance in the competition until 1992.

Don Fox missed a last-gasp kick in the 1968 Challenge Cup final that would have won the match for Wakefield

Trinity. As Leeds fans celebrated and Fox sank to his
knees commentator Eddie Wareing summed up his
desperation with: *"He's a poor lad"*, words that have
become as famous as the moment itself.

The ninth World Cup competition stretched over three
years, with certain matches from Test series already
scheduled between the countries counting towards the
final table. This format was difficult to follow, however,
and it was only once the knockout stages had been
reached that crowds warmed to the event.

In 1995 and 2000 an emerging nations tournament was
held alongside the World Cup. It was first won by the
Cook Islands, with the British Amateur Rugby League
Association winning in 2000.

Australian rugby league player Jamie Ainscough thought
he'd picked up an infection in his arm after a game in
2002, but an X-ray revealed England's Martin Gleeson
had left a tooth embedded in his flesh after an accidental
collision!

The 2000 World Cup tournament suffered due to a
number of mismatches in the group stages. The RFL lost
money thanks to low spectator numbers and would not
recover until 2004.

Australian Wendell Sailor scored two tries in the Rugby
League World Cup final against New Zealand at Old
Trafford, Manchester, in 2000, which his team went on to
win by 40-12. Having swapped codes, he was on the

losing side (17-20) when Australia met England in the final of the 2003 RWC in Sydney.

Sixteen-year-old Australian rugby league forward Bilal Elzamtar was banned from the sport for 30 years for kicking and punching a touch judge who disallowed a try in 2005.

Australian rugby league winger John Hopoate was found guilty of interfering with the opposition after three North Queensland players testified that he'd deliberately inserted his fingers into their backsides during a game in 2001.

Australian five-eighth Trent Barrett had a hand in three of his side's tries as they beat Great Britain to the Tri-Nations final in 2005. However, he had a bizarre match in that he was sin-binned twice!

The Challenge Cup Final replay between Warrington and Halifax (18-4) at the Odsal stadium in Bradford in 1954 recorded an attendance of 102,575, a figure that still stands today as the largest ever for a league match. Some newspaper reports claim that a further 20,000 spectators got in free after a section of fence collapsed.

"I don't like this new law because your first instinct when you see a man on the ground is to go down on him"
Murray Mexted

"There's one more rugby league result to give you, just to put the jigsaw into focus"
Andy Peebles

CLUB RUGBY LEAGUE

THE SUPER LEAGUE (EUROPE)

This was formed in 1996 and backed by Rupert Murdoch so he could bargain with Kerry Packer during the so-called Super League war over broadcasting rights. For the first two years the league leaders at the end of the season were declared champions but from 1998 onwards the top six of the 12 teams (who all play each other on a home and away basis during the regular season) entered the play-offs, with the two best teams meeting in the Grand Final at Old Trafford, Manchester. (A League Leader's Shield is presented as a minor trophy to the best team before the play-offs begin.)

THE CHALLENGE CUP

This is one of the country's most prestigious sporting trophies. It was held at Wembley from 1929, when Wigan beat Dewsbury 13-2, until 1999, when Leeds Rhinos beat the London Broncos 52-16, before the old stadium was torn down to make way for the new home of British sport. The final has since travelled round the country to Murrayfield, the Millennium Stadium and even Twickenham. Since 1946 the man-of-the-match has been

"That's a very handy kick on his unfamiliar leg"
Australian commentator

awarded the Lance Todd Trophy (voted for by the Rugby League Writers' Association) at a celebratory dinner at The Willows, home of the Salford City Reds. The trophy was named in honour of the New Zealand born player who was tragically killed in a road accident during the Second World War.

Wigan have appeared in 27 finals, winning 17, including eight in a row between 1988 and 1995. This included a cup-run of 43 unbeaten matches. Shaun Edwards made ten final appearances for them and 11 overall, winning nine and losing just two: 1984 with Wigan and 1999 with the London Broncos.

THE WORLD CLUB CHALLENGE

This competition pits the winners of the European Super League against the winners of the Australian National Rugby League. Though it is supposed to be held alternately in Australia and Britain, it has remained in the UK since 2000. British clubs have won the title eight times and Australian five since the competition's inception in 1976. Only since 2000 has the match been played yearly. Leeds Rhinos beat the Canterbury Bulldogs 39-32 in the 2005 final.

THE NATIONAL RUGBY LEAGUE (NRL)

Born out of the New South Wales Rugby League, which ran from 1908 to 1994, and the Australian Rugby League (1995-1997), the NRL combines 15 teams from Australia and New Zealand in a similar competition to the European Super League. They play each other in a rotating roster that lasts for 26 weeks, known as the 'regular season', where teams play once against teams in their

GRAND FINAL WINNERS

Year	Champions	Runners up
1998	Wigan Warriors	Leeds Rhinos
1999	St Helens	Bradford Bulls
2000	St Helens	Wigan Warriors
2001	Bradford Bulls	Wigan Warriors
2002	St Helens	Bradford Bulls
2003	Bradford Bulls	Wigan Warriors
2004	Leeds Rhinos	Bradford Bulls
2005	Bradford Bulls	Leeds Rhinos
2006		
2007		

group and twice against the others. The top eight teams qualify, then play in a series of elimination matches with the best two meeting in the Grand Final in Sydney. The Wests Tigers are the current champions having defeated the North Queensland Cowboys 30-16 in the 2005 final.

STATE OF ORIGIN

This annual three Test series between the Queensland Maroons and the New South Wales Blues was first held in 1908. It is now so popular that the television coverage regularly rakes in the top three audiences nationwide. To be eligible, a player must have started his representative rugby career in one of the two states, though, until 1979 he represented the state his club was in not the state he

Score	League Leaders	Crowd
10-4	Wigan Warriors	75,000
8-6	Bradford Bulls	50,717
29-16	Wigan Warriors	60,164
37-6	Bradford Bulls	60,000
19-18	St Helens	61,138
25-12	Bradford Bulls	65,537
16-8	Leeds Rhinos	67,000
15-6	St Helens	65,738

was born in. New South Wales dominated the early clashes, winning 75% of all matches before 1956 and over 90% until 1980. Since the change in format in 1980 New South Wales have won 37 matches, Queensland 36, and there have been two draws.

"You don't like to see hookers going down on players like that"
Murray Mexted

"Every time he gets the ball he moves around like a banana-shaped umbrella to cut the park off"
Alex Murphy

"And you can't take your eyes off this game without seeing something happen"
Harry Gration

MONEY MATTERS

1871: The joining fee and annual subscription to the RFU are set at five shillings.

1872: William Webb Ellis leaves £9000 to charity in his will.

1879: Hawick versus Melrose attracts a 5000 crowd and brings gate receipts of £63.

1880: The RFU agree to pay travelling expenses for international matches.

1886: Footballers and cricketers receive compensation for time taken off work to compete. Rugby players do not.

1887: Bradford pay Blackheath £4 per player to secure a game.

1888: Lions' captain Andrew Stoddart receives £200 in expenses. Halifax player J.P. Clowes accepts £15 to buy equipment before joining the British touring party to Australia, who are collectively paid expenses and match fees. They also play a number of Australian Rules matches to boost their income.

1892: Two clubs in Yorkshire pay their players compensation for missing work.

1893: Yorkshire clubs propose that mill workers and miners are paid six shilling 'broken time' allowances for missing Saturday's work. David and Evan James, both Welsh internationals, are suspended for receiving such compensation.

1895: The Northern Union allows players to receive compensation and splits from the RFU.

1900-1995: Hundreds of Welsh players are lured to rugby league sides in the north of England because they can't officially be paid to play union.

1907: William Williams buys 10 acres of market garden at Twickenham for £5572. It becomes known as Billy's cabbage patch.

1908: The touring Australian rugby union side are paid three shillings a day for 'out-of-pocket' expenses. On their return home, 13 players join league teams and turn professional.

1917: Australian rugby league club Glebe strike in protest at not being allowed to field a player from outside their recruiting zone. The league suspends them for more than six months.

1919-1930: Australasian league players are lured to Britain by higher wages.

1921: Harold Buck transfers from Hunslet to Leeds for £1000. Featherstone Rovers become a fully professional team.

1927: Challenge Cup Final broadcast by the BBC.

1930: France are suspended from the Five Nations Championship because the RFU believes they are paying their players. They won't be reinstated until 1947.

1948: Wigan versus Bradford becomes first televised league match.

1956: The New South Wales state government legalises the playing of poker machines in clubs. This revenue becomes the main source of income for league teams.

1960: BBC controller David Attenborough decides to screen matches, enabling clubs to make money from the broadcasting rights.

1977: The British Lions play the Barbarians with the

proceeds going to the Jubilee Trust Fund. The match raises £100,000, the largest individual contribution.

1983: Reporter Chris Masters finds deep seated corruption within the Australian league game. Some officials are jailed for siphoning funds from clubs.

1987: First Rugby World Cup makes a profit of £1 million on commercial income of £3.3 million.

1990s: The battle for control of broadcasting rights affects clubs the world over and ends with the Super League war between Rupert Murdoch and Kerry Packer.

1991: England rugby union players form their own company to safeguard their commercial activities during the World Cup. They clear about £1000 each.

1992: Martin Offiah leaves Widnes for Wigan in a world record £440,000 transfer.

1994: Top union players clear £6000 after negotiating deals with sponsors and the media. Australian World Cup squad sign a deal worth £35,000 per man for the 1995 tournament.

1995: Rugby union turns professional. Some high profile players, including those who have never played the other code, switch allegiance.

"Neil Baker is standing on the touchline with his hands in his tracksuit bottoms scratching his head"
Graham McGarry

"Nathan Grey has got the ball on a piece of string. I'll qualify that by saying it's a rickety piece of string"
Australian commentator

1996: Rupert Murdoch's money backs the European Super League, which signs to BSkyB.

1999: Bristol lead the way in trying to sign Jonah Lomu. They table a £1.1 million bid that does not breach the £1.8 million wage cap imposed by the premier league. Clubs face a £3 fine for every £1 they exceed the cap, and a ban from European competition if the total runs to more than £100,000.

2000: The Rugby League World Cup turns a huge loss as spectators stay away from the mismatched group games.

2003: Organisers of the Rugby Union World Cup enjoy a £64 million surplus after the tournament. The RWC website attracts 495 million hits during the event. The Australian economy is boosted by nearly a billion dollars. Jonny Wilkinson's earnings predicted to be £20 million over next five years.

2004: The Rugby Football League finally clears a profit after the World Cup debacle. Player numbers increase 94% in two years as a result.

2005: Australian NRL records increased crowd numbers, 39% increase in sponsorship and a 41% increase in merchandising royalties. English Super League clubs may spend no more than £1.7 million per year on wages, or about £40,000 per player. RFU invests £1.6 million in youth development schemes. 500,000 players and officials are covered for up to £250,000 in the event of injury. Top premiership players reported to be earning £250,000 per year.

2006: Union players in New Zealand demand 40% wage increase. Some players starting on $20,000 are offered $65,000 to swap clubs. Wage cap set at $2 million per club.

RUGBY ON FILM

Three and a half minutes of film survive from the England-New Zealand match at Crystal Palace in 1905. It is believed to be the oldest footage in existence.

In 1972 a plane carrying a representative Uruguayan team crashed in the Andes. The survivors lived for 72 days by eating the players killed in the crash. The story was transferred to the big screen in 1993, with the release of the film *Alive* starring Ethan Hawke. Twenty years after the original crash, documentary makers caught up with the hero, Nando Parrado, and the rest of the team. Piers Paul Read's book of the same name lends much greater weight to the story.

Tom Brown's School Days, about his formative years at Rugby School, was filmed in 1950. Though the story takes place in about 1834, no one manages to pick up the ball and run in the rugby scenes.

Richard Harris starred in *This Sporting Life* (1963), playing a gritty rugby league player determined to get in the local side. Though there are only about fifteen minutes of rugby footage, the scenes are powerful, both emotionally and physically.

An all-star British cast (Neil Morrissey, Samantha Janus, Gryff Rhys Jones, Gary Olsen, Tony Slattery) made *Up'n'Under* (1998) a feel-good comedy about an awful Wheatsheaf Arms sevens side taking on the mighty Cobbler's Arms. The side have no motivation to train, and are quite happy quaffing beers in the pub, until they are introduced to a gorgeous fitness instructor (Janus).

The Kiwis tried their hand at comedy with *Old Scores* (1991) about the death-bed confession of a Welsh touch judge, who admitted he'd cheated to help his side beat the All Blacks in 1966. It is decided that the only way to settle the result is to replay the fixture in 1991 with all the players from the original match. All Black legend Waka Nathan makes an appearance, as does Welshman Phil Bennett.

Exiles (1999) is a Canadian film about the captain of the Minneapolis Exiles trying to win the SNAFU cup in Winnipeg, a trophy he has always dreamed of holding. Unfortunately, the team's coach is detained by customs and the captain must then lead his team of misfits to the game.

Asini (1999) follows 40-year-old Italo from Milan as he is forced to give up the sport and takes up a post as a gymnastics teacher in a school instead.

"Ouch! Well, that's the ultimate dummy scissors I guess"
Nigel Starmer-Smith describes a French back-line move
that ends with Alain Penaud and Jean-Luc Sadourny
colliding painfully

"I had visions of spending the rest of my life doing pizza adverts"
England lock Ben Kay reflects on missing out on a certain
try in the 2003 RWC final when he dropped the ball just
short of the line

The following sources were particularly helpful while writing this book:

www.rugbyfootballhistory.com
www.rwc2003.irb.com
www.bbc.co.uk/wales
www.barbarianfc.co.uk
www.answers.com
www.nrl.com
www.seniority.co.uk
www.wikipedia.org
www.google.co.uk
Classic Rugby Clangers by David Mortimer
Muddied Oafs by Richard Beard
Rugby's Strangest Matches by John Griffiths

I would also like to thank Simon Metcalf, Tony Bowden, Seamus McCann, Darren Thompson and Rachel Harrison for their invaluable contributions.

If I hadn't listened to my cousin's advice
I would never have settled down to write.
This book is dedicated to the memory of Sophie Warne